THE VEGAN SLOW COOKER COOKBOOK

38 Easy To Prepare Vegan Recipes For Your Slow Cooker

Martha Drummond

Table of Contents

Introduction:

Are you tired of spending all your time slaving away in the kitchen trying to whip together delicious vegan recipes? If so, you need to get out your slow cooker. Using a slow cooker can save you a whole lot of time while allowing you to fix tasty, healthy vegan recipes for the whole family. Whether you are looking for main dish recipes, easy breakfast ideas or the perfect vegan desserts, you will find all the best vegan friendly slow cooker recipes in this recipe book. Along with great recipes, you will also find some great slow cooker tips that you can use to make the most of your slow cooker, ensuring that your recipes turn out wonderfully when you make them. Get ready to start using your slow cooker more than ever while cooking up taste bud tempting dishes that you will enjoy making repeatedly.

Chapter 1: Vegan Recipes and Slow Cooking – The Benefits

Eating a vegan diet is about far more than animal rights, as some individuals mistakenly think. Many vegans are passionate about animal rights, but the vegan diet offers many important benefits beyond championing the rights of animals. Following a well-balanced vegan diet offers many excellent health benefits and using a slow cooker to cook delicious vegan meals offers even more excellent benefits that you and your family can enjoy. Here is a closer look at some of the top benefits of eating a vegan diet, the benefits of cooking with a slow cooker and some essential tips and tricks you can use for slow cooking success.

Benefits of Eating Vegan

Choosing a vegan diet provides you with a variety of excellent health benefits. Here are just a few of the excellent health benefits you can enjoy if you begin following a vegan diet.

- Benefit #1 – Cancer Prevention – One of the main benefits of eating a vegan diet is cancer prevention. The vegetables that make up a large portion of the vegan diet include high amounts of phytochemicals, which happens to have anti-cancer properties. Studies show that eating a vegan diet can help prevent many cancers, including prostate cancer, ovarian cancer, breast cancer and colon cancer. Some research has even shown that individuals eating a vegan diet are 40% less likely to end up with cancer.

- Benefit #2 – Reduce Blood Pressure and Cholesterol – Eating a vegan diet can also help to reduce your blood pressure and cholesterol levels. Since a vegan diet is rich in whole grains, it can help to reduce blood pressure. By eliminating foods that come from animals, dietary cholesterol is eliminated from your diet, which helps lower levels of bad cholesterol. Reducing blood pressure and cholesterol levels is extremely beneficial to your overall health and may even help you enjoy increased longevity.

- Benefit #3 – Reduce Risk of Heart Disease – You can also benefit from a reduced risk of heart disease when eating a vegan diet. Studies have shown that eating a vegan diet can help to reduce your risk of heart disease, reducing the risk of strokes and heart attacks. By reducing blood pressure and cholesterol, it is possible to improve heart health and keep heart disease at bay.

- Benefit #4 – Prevent Diabetes – Type 2 diabetes is a common problem today and it is becoming more prevalent, even among children and teens. Eating a vegan diet can help to prevent diabetes, since the diet focuses on complex carbs and high fiber foods, helping the body better use the insulin that it produces. When eating a vegan diet and combining it with exercise, many individuals have found that they were able to reverse many of the effects of Type 2 diabetes, controlling blood sugar by diet and exercise alone.

- Benefit #5 – Improved Nutrition – A vegan diet is full of healthy foods like whole grains, soy products, fresh fruits, fresh veggies, beans and nuts. Eating these healthy foods instead of eating processed and animal foods can improve overall nutrition. Following a vegan diet can help to reduce saturated fats in your diet and includes complex carbohydrates. The diet is high in fiber as well, which helps to fight colon cancer and ensure you have healthy bowel movements. While eating a vegan diet, you will enjoy a better intake of vitamins, minerals and phtyochemicals as well.

- Benefit #6 – Healthy, Lean Body – Not only does a vegan diet provide better nutrition and disease prevention, but it also offers you the benefit of a healthy, lean body. Many individuals on a vegan diet find that it is easier to maintain a healthy weight, they enjoy a lower body mass index and have high energy levels. Some studies show that eating a vegan diet may lead to longer life and it also results in healthy nails, hair and skin.

Of course, these are only a few of the excellent benefits you can enjoy when you begin eating a vegan diet. Other important benefits many people enjoy when eating vegan include a reduction in allergies, reduced migraines, a reduced chance of osteoporosis and a reduction in the symptoms of arthritis.

Benefits of Using Your Slow Cooker

If you lead a busy lifestyle, cooking with a slow cooker may change your life. Sometimes it is difficult to get a healthy, vegan meal on the table when you do not have a lot of time. Using your slow cooker to cook meals can make a huge difference, offering many benefits. If you are not familiar with all the advantages that your slow cooker has to offer, it is time to give it a try. Here are just a few of the benefits you can enjoy when you start cooking delicious vegan recipes in your slow cooker.

- Benefit#1 – Make Healthier Food Choices – One of the benefits of using your slow cooker is that it makes it easier for you to make healthier food choices. Using your slow cooker makes it easy to whip up healthy, vegan meals in no time. You need little fat or oil when cooking in your slow cooker, since you do not have to worry about your ingredients sticking to the slow cooker. As you need to plan slow cooker meals in advance, you can pay better attention to what you are eating, ensuring you focus on healthy foods for your body.

- Benefit #2 – No Need to Tend Food – Another great benefit of using your slow cooker is that you have no need to stay in the kitchen to tend the food while it is cooking. This makes it easy for you to put dinner in the slow cooker, going about other tasks while the food cooks without your help. For busy individuals that do not have time to stay in the kitchen for an hour cooking, a slow cooker is a fabulous choice.

- Benefit #3 – Keeps the Kitchen Cool – Although many people immediately associate using a slow cooker with warm winter meals, the truth is that you can use your slow cooker in the summer months to keep your kitchen cool. When it is hot outside, the last thing you want to do is turn on the oven, which often makes your kitchen even hotter. The slow cooker does not give off a lot of heat, allowing you to cook up a warm, nutritious, vegan meal without heating up the kitchen further.

- Benefit #4 – Save Time and Work – Using a slow cooker will also save you a lot of time and work. All you have to do is the prep work for the recipe and then you throw everything in the slow cooker and let it do all the work for you. You will save a lot of time, since you can easily take care of other tasks while the slow cooker cooks up a nice meal. In fact, you can set it to have dinner ready when you come in the door at night, so you will not have to worry about spending time in the kitchen trying to whip up a meal after a long day. Slow cooker recipes are also fairly simple, so you do not have to work hard to get these recipes prepared and ready to start cooking.

- Benefit #5 – Reduce Kitchen Energy Usage – When you use a slow cooker, you are using a lot less energy than you would if you were cooking on your electric oven. Slow cookers only use a small amount of energy, so you will reduce your kitchen energy usage by using a slow cooker on a regular basis.

- Benefit #6 – Cleanup is Easy – Cleanup is super easy with a slow cooker, which is another big benefit you will enjoy when you begin cooking with your slow cooker. While you may dirty a few things during the recipe prep, after you eat the meal, you will only need to clean up the slow cooker, saving you a lot of time. Instead of dealing with a lot of pots and pans, you only need to clean up a single pot and you are done.

- Benefit #7 – Great Distribution of Flavor – Cooking in a slow cooker also offers the benefit of great distribution of flavor. It gently and slowly heats up foods, allowing plenty of time for the flavors to spread throughout the entire dish, resulting in tasty, flavorful dishes.

Slow Cooking Tips and Tricks

Slow cookers, often called crock pots, cook foods at low temperatures for 4-12 hours, in most cases. A consistent temperature is maintained by the slow cooker, which results in delicious, moist food. Since the slow cooker uses low temperatures to cook the food, it is possible to use long cooking times without worrying about burning foods. Slow cookers are perfect for cooking stews, soups, main dishes, desserts and sides, and it is easy to prepare foods the night before, then placing them in the heating unit to cook the next day. To help you enjoy all the benefits a slow cooker has to offer, here are a few slow cooking tips and tricks you will definitely want to remember for the best results.

Choose the Right Slow Cooker

First, it is very important that you choose the right slow cooker for your needs. For most of the recipes in this book, a round slow cooker will work perfectly. You will find that several different sizes are available when you are ready to purchase a slow cooker. For a family, four quart slow cookers work well for a family of four, while five or six quart slow cookers will work best for larger families. It is also important to ensure you choose a sturdy, high quality slow cooker that will provide you with delicious meals.

Avoid Overfilling the Slow Cooker

Another important slow cooking tip to remember is to avoid overfilling the slow cooker when you use it. It is usually best to avoid filling the slow cooker more than 2/3 of the way full, although this may vary depending on the brand of slow cooker that you purchase. If you overfill the slow cooker, it could make your meal take longer to cook and your food may not cook completely, causing a food safety hazard.

Remember to Keep the Lid On

When you cook with a slow cooker, it is tempting to open the lid to check out your cooking meal from time to time. However, it is important that you keep the lid on while the slow cooker is cooking. When you open the lid, it allows a lot of heat to escape from the cooker, which will make it take longer for your food to finish cooking. For every time you open the lid, it will require you to cook the food another 20 minutes to reach the desired doneness. The only times you should open up the lid is to check doneness when the meal is almost done.

Plan Ahead to Save Time

To save on time, plan those meals ahead of time. Just a bit of planning can save you a huge amount of time. For example, you can prepare ingredients for meals the night before so you simply need to toss them into the slow cooker the next morning to get your meal started. Just a little planning and preparation can go a long way when you are cooking with a slow cooker.

Consider Using Slow Cooker Liners

Another excellent tip to remember is to consider using slow cooker liners if you want to make slow cooking even more convenient. Slow cooker liners are plastic liners designed to withstand the heat of your slow cooker. All you have to do is place the liner in the slow cooker before you add the food. Then, when you are done with the meal, you simply throw the liner away and you do not have to worry about cleaning out the slow cooker. It makes cleanup a breeze and saves you a lot of time.

Know Low and High Setting Conversions

You also need to know the low and high setting conversions to make the most of your slow cooker. For example, if a slow cooker recipe tells you to cook the food for 3 hours on high, you may want to slow down the cooking so the recipe isn't ready until later. On the other hand, the recipe may require you to cook the recipe for 8 hours on low, and you may want to speed that time up. The rule of thumb is to add or subtract four hours if you want to change between the high and low settings. For example, if the recipe calls for 3 hours on high, add 4 hours if you want to cook it on low, making the time 7 hours. If the recipe requires you to cook the food for 10 hours on low and you want it done faster, subtract 4 hours to cook it on high, which means you'll need to cook the recipe for 6 hours on the high setting.

Avoid Using Frozen Ingredients

It is best to avoid using frozen ingredients in your slow cooker for the best food safety. If the food is frozen, it will take longer to cook, which could be a problem. Frozen vegetables or other frozen ingredients should be thawed out before you use them in the slow cooker.

Don't Add Too Much Liquid

Lastly, make sure that you do not add too much liquid when you are cooking in the slow cooker. Since the lid is closed the entire time you are cooking in a slow cooker, there is little evaporation of liquids when compared to cooking in an oven or on the stovetop. You will notice that most recipes for a slow cooker will call for about half the liquid called for in a conventional recipe. Do not be tempted to add extra liquid or you may ruin the recipe.

Cooking with your slow cooker can be a lot of fun. With these helpful tips and tricks, you'll get the best results from these delicious slow cooker, vegan recipes.

Chapter 2: Vegan Slow Cooker Breakfast Recipes

Most people do not think about using their slow cooker for breakfast, but it is actually possible to whip up some delicious, easy recipes for breakfast dishes using your slow cooker. The best part about these recipes is that you usually can put them in the slow cooker the night before and have breakfast ready when you get up in the morning. From delicious bread pudding French toast, to scrumptious multigrain and apple hot cereal, to a yummy coconut and orange vegan oatmeal recipe, your family is sure to enjoy these tasty, easy vegan breakfast recipes as you start your day.

❧Cinnamon Pumpkin Vegan Oatmeal❧

This delicious vegan oatmeal recipe has all the goodness of pumpkin pie, but it is a healthy way to start your day without any guilt. Set your slow cooker timer to cook this up during the night so you can dig into this oatmeal for breakfast the next morning. You can even make a huge batch on the weekend and then reheat servings throughout the week for a quick, easy, tasty breakfast.

What You'll Need:

- 6 cups of water
- 1 tablespoon of pumpkin pie spice
- 1 ½ cups of steel-cut oats
- 1 cup of brown sugar
- 2 tablespoons of cinnamon
- 1 can (15oz) of pure pumpkin puree

How to Make It:

Spray the slow cooker with nonstick cooking spray. In the prepared slow cooker, stir together the brown sugar, pumpkin pie spice, cinnamon, oats, water and the pumpkin puree. Make sure it is well combined.

Cover and set the slow cooker to low, allowing it to cook for about six hours.

Be sure to thoroughly stir up the oatmeal again before you serve it.

Serve warm with toppings of your choice or some non-dairy, vegan milk.

Servings:

Makes 6 servings.

❧Bread Pudding French Toast Vegan Recipe❧

This delicious recipe is the perfect blend of French toast and bread pudding, making a great breakfast dish. It's a wonderful idea as well if you have guests coming over for brunch on the weekend. This recipe combines the best of sweetness and spices, and it is sweet enough that you will not even need to add more syrup, unless you are a syrup addict.

What You'll Need:

- 6 ounces of silken tofu, thoroughly drained
- ¼ cup of pecans, coarsely chopped
- 8 cups of soft Italian bread, cut into cubes
- 1 tablespoon of vegan butter
- ½ cup of light brown sugar, packed
- 2 cups of plain non-dairy milk
- 2 teaspoons of vanilla
- 1/8 teaspoon of allspice
- ¼ cup of pure maple syrup (more for serving if desired)
- ¼ teaspoon of salt
- ¼ teaspoon of ground nutmeg
- 1 teaspoon of ground cinnamon

How to Make It:

The night before, place cubed bread on a baking sheet and toast at 275F for about 30 minutes, drying the bread cubes.

Spray the slow cooker with some cooking spray. Place dried bread cubes in the slow cooker.

Meanwhile, add vanilla, nutmeg, salt, brown sugar, cinnamon, allspice and tofu to a food processor. Process until well blended. Add maple syrup and milk, processing shortly to blend in the liquid ingredients.

Pour the milk mixture over the cubes of bread, using a wooden spoon to press the mixture to make sure all the bread is moistened. Top with bits of vegan butter, then sprinkle the chopped pecans on top.

Cover the slow cooker and turn on high. Cook for 90-100 minutes until the bread pudding is firm.

Serve warm with more maple syrup if desired.

Servings:

Makes 8 small servings or 4 large servings.

❧Coconut Milk Yogurt Vegan Slow Cooker Recipe❧

Just because you are eating vegan does not mean that you cannot enjoy delicious yogurt. This recipe teaches you how to make your own delicious vegan yogurt using your slow cooker. You'll enjoy this delicious yogurt and you can always add fun toppings to the yogurt for extra flavor, such as honey, nuts or your favorite fruit.

What You'll Need:

- 4 tablespoons of Agar Agar Flakes
- ½ gallon of coconut milk (unsweetened)
- 1 6-oz container of plain, coconut milk yogurt (dairy free)

How to make It:

The night before, mix the coconut milk and the Agar Agar flakes together in your slow cooker.

Turn the slow cooker on low, then cover the mixture and allow to cook on low for about an hour.

After an hour, take off the lid and whisk the mixture again, making sure it is fully incorporated. Cover again and allow it to cook for 1.5 more hours.

Now, take the lid off again, whisking together the milk and agar, adding the lid back to the slow cooker and unplugging it. With the lid on, allow the mixture to sit in the warm crockpot for three hours.

After three hours, take out about two cups of the mixture, placing in a bowl. Add in the coconut milk yogurt, using a whisk to whisk together the mixture until combined, then place back in the crockpot. Stir again to combine all ingredients.

The slow cooker should still be unplugged. Cover with the lid, then wrap the slow cooker with a couple of bath towels to insulate it and keep it warm.

Allow the mixture to sit overnight (10-12 hours). In the morning, you will have a thick, yogurt mixture.

To add extra thickness, you can always add about ¼ cup of arrowroot powder or tapioca to the mixture.

Refrigerate the vegan yogurt.

Serve cold with your favorite toppings.

Servings:

Makes about ½ gallon of yogurt.

❧Coconut and Orange Vegan Oatmeal❧

This tasty recipe combines the goodness of coconut milk with delicious orange flavors, giving you an oatmeal recipe that will tempt your taste buds in the morning. You can always top the oatmeal with fresh mandarin slices when you serve it to add extra orange flavor. You can also add more sweetener to your own taste.

What You'll Need:

- 4 cups of coconut milk, unsweetened
- 2-4 tablespoons of sweetener of choice
- 2/3 cup of coconut, finely shredded
- 1 cup of steel cut oats
- Orange zest as a garnish
- 2 teaspoons of orange extract
- Can of mandarin oranges, drained, for topping (if desired)

How to Make It:

The night before, use some cooking spray to spray the slow cooker.

Add the coconut milk, coconut, oats and orange extract to the slow cooker. Mix together and then cover with the lid.

Cook for 7-9 hours on low overnight.

The next morning, turn off the cooker and stir the oatmeal.

Add sweetener to your own taste.

Serve up the oatmeal in bowls, topping with the orange zest and the mandarin oranges if desired.

Enjoy while warm.

Servings:

Makes 4-6 servings.

❧Vegan Multigrain and Apple Hot Cereal❧

Packed with all the goodness of wheat berries, steel cut oats, brown rice and quinoa, this hot cereal is packed with fiber that will keep you full all day long, making it a perfect breakfast recipe. Not only is it extremely healthy, but it is very easy to make as well. If you end up with leftovers, you can easily reheat the leftovers to enjoy the breakfast on another day as well. While it calls for apples, you could always substitute in another favorite fruit for something different.

What You'll Need:

- ½ cup of steel cut oats
- ½ cup of brown rice (rinsed and then drained)
- ½ cup of wheat berries
- ½ cup of quinoa, (rinsed and then drained)
- 1 apple, washed, peeled, cored and then diced
- 1 teaspoon of cinnamon
- 5.5 cups of water
- 1 teaspoon of vanilla
- Additional dried fruit (if desired)

How to Make It:

Lightly grease the slow cooker or coat with cooking spray.

Place oats, rice, wheat berries, quinoa, apple, cinnamon, water and vanilla in the slow cooker. Mix together to combine ingredients.

Cover and cook on low heat for 6-7 hours.

About an hour before you serve the oatmeal, you can add additional dried fruit if you desire, such as cranberries or raisins.

Cover and cook for the remaining hour.

Serve up oatmeal while hot, topping with a bit of brown sugar, honey or some syrup for sweetness.

Servings:

Makes 6 1-cup servings.

❧Easy Overnight Maple and Brown Sugar Vegan Oatmeal❧

This overnight recipe for vegan maple and brown sugar oatmeal is perfect for a nice brunch on the weekend. It is wonderful to be able to mix it all up the night before, allowing it to cook while you are fast asleep. Not only is it easy to make, but it is wonderfully tasty as well. Just make sure that you do use the steel cut oats, since you are cooking the oatmeal for a long time. Quick oats just will not hold up to the slow cooker very well.

What You'll Need:

- ¼ cup of maple syrup, pure
- 2 cups of steel cut oats
- 1 teaspoon of cinnamon
- 6-8 cups of water (adjust for the consistency you want)
- ½ teaspoon of salt
- ¼ cup of brown sugar, packed

How to Make It:

The night before, use some non-stick cooking spray to spray the slow cooker.

Add the syrup, oats, cinnamon, water, salt and brown sugar to the slow cooker. Stir the ingredients to combine them.

Cover and cook on the low setting for about 8 hours.

In the morning, unplug the slow cooker and stir it well, which will help it thicken up.

Allow it to sit covered for 5-10 minutes before serving.

Serve warm with some additional brown sugar and fresh fruit of your choice. You can also add a bit of coconut milk if desired.

Servings:

Makes 6-8 servings.

Chapter 3: Vegan Slow Cooker Main Course Recipes

You may be surprised at how many delicious main dishes you can whip up in your slow cooker. The great thing about using your slow cooker is that you can easily place your food in the slow cooker to cook throughout the day, which means it will be ready for you to eat at dinner time. Whether you are in the mood for a delicious vegan curry recipe or a vegan enchilada dish that will please the entire family, you will find the best main dishes right here in this chapter. From Italian themed dishes to an amazing, easy recipe for vegan tamales, get ready to enjoy some incredible foods.

❧Tasty Vegan Peanut Butter Satay❧

If you love Thai food, you've probably enjoyed peanut butter satay before, a delicious spicy, sweet peanut sauce that is incredibly tasty. This is a variation of satay, but it is completely vegan. It is full of delicious Thai flavors, including pure peanut butter, stewed tomatoes, chili paste, garlic and lime juice. This will definitely make dinner a huge hit in your house.

What You'll Need:

- 6 cloves of minced garlic
- 1 1/3 cup of all-natural peanut butter
- 1 large sweet onion, chopped
- 6 tablespoons of brown sugar
- 1 ½ cups of water
- 15 oz of canned stewed tomatoes
- 2 teaspoons of chili paste
- 2 red or green bell peppers, chopped
- 2 limes, juiced
- 2 tablespoons of Bragg's Liquid Aminos

How to Make It:

In the slow cooker, combine the garlic, peanut butter, onion, brown sugar, water, tomatoes, chili paste, peppers and Bragg's Liquid Aminos, mixing together until well combined.

Cover the slow cooker and turn on high, allowing to cook for 3-4 hours.

Before serving, stir the lime juice into the satay, adding a bit more water if the satay is too thick.

Serve while hot. Enjoy!

Servings:

Makes 4 servings.

❧Spinach and Mushroom Vegan Marinara Sauce❧

If you want to enjoy Italian food without spending a lot of time working in the kitchen, this delicious marinara sauce is sure to please. It is packed with delicious veggies and combines spicy tomato with sweet flavors as well. You can easily adjust the garlic, pepper and salt to taste, ending up with a delicious sauce to serve up over your favorite pasta.

What You'll Need:

- 1 pack of chopped, frozen spinach (10 oz), thawed completely and drained
- 1 onion, roughly chopped
- 1 can of sliced mushrooms (4.5 oz), well drained
- 2 tablespoons of dried oregano
- 1 can of crushed tomatoes, including liquid (28 oz)
- ¼ cup of olive oil
- 3 cans of tomato paste (6 oz)
- 5 cloves of garlic, finely minced
- 2 tablespoons of salt
- 2 ½ tablespoons of crushed red pepper
- 2 tablespoons of dried basil
- 2 bay leaves
- 1/3 cup of carrot, grated

How to Make It:

Combine the carrot, tomato paste, crushed red pepper, tomatoes, olive oil, mushrooms, bay leaves, onion, basil, salt, spinach, garlic and oregano in the slow cooker. Mix together until the ingredients are well combined.

Cover with the lid, cooking for 4 hours on high.

Remove lid and stir well.

Cover and turn heat down to low, cooking for 2 more hours.

Remove bay leaves and serve sauce over hot pasta. Enjoy immediately.

Servings:

Makes 8 servings.

❧Slow Cooker Coconut Vegan Curry❧

This adaptation of traditional coconut curry is completely vegan and full of flavor. When you make it you will delight in this creamy curry that is perfect over rice or even by itself. The touch of hot pepper adds just a bit of heat, but if you do not want the spiciness, you can always omit the cayenne pepper from the recipe. This curry recipe also packs in delicious veggies, making it a healthy main dish that the entire family will appreciate.

What You'll Need:

- ¼ cup of curry powder
- 1 package of dry onion soup mix (1 oz package)
- ½ teaspoon of red pepper flakes
- 1 cup of green peas
- 1 can of coconut cream (14 oz)
- 5 russet potatoes, washed, peeled and cut into cubes (1-inch cubes)
- 1 ½ cups of carrots, matchstick cut
- 1 tablespoon of chili powder
- ¼ cup of fresh cilantro, chopped
- ½ teaspoon of cayenne pepper (if desired)
- Water (as needed)
- 1 red bell pepper, sliced
- 1 green bell pepper, sliced
- 2 tablespoons of flour

How to Make It:

In the bottom of the slow cooker, place all the cubed potatoes.

In a small bowl, mix together the flour, cayenne pepper, curry powder, red pepper flakes and the chili powder.

Sprinkle the curry mixture over the cubed potatoes.

Carefully stir up the potatoes to make sure they are evenly coated with the curry mixture.

Add the green bell pepper, coconut cream, red bell pepper and onion soup mix. Stir thoroughly until ingredients are well combined.

Place the lid on the slow cooker, cooking for 3-4 hours on low until the mixture begins to bubble. If needed, add water to ensure the mixture stays moist.

Add carrots to the curry, allowing to cook for 30 more minutes.

Add the peas, cooking for about 30 more minutes, ensuring that the veggies are tender.

Serve over warm rice while hot, garnishing with chopped cilantro.

Servings:

Makes 8 servings.

Vegan Spaghetti Bolognaise Sauce

This sauce tastes exactly like bolognaise, but it uses soybeans instead of any meat. The sauce is wonderful on its own, but it can be used to top rice or pasta as well. You will love all the incredible flavors that mix together to make this sauce, and it is packed with delicious veggies, so it makes a healthy dinner.

What You'll Need:

- 1 cup of black olives, pitted
- ¼ cup of olive oil
- 2 cups of soybeans, dried
- 1 cup of green olives, pitted
- 2 tablespoons of dried basil
- ½ teaspoon of pepper
- 1 cup of red wine
- 4 large tomatoes, cut in wedges
- 2 cans of tomato paste (6oz)
- 1 large onion, finely chopped
- 3 cans of diced tomatoes (14.5 oz)
- 1 can of whole kernel corn, well drained (11 oz)
- 4 tablespoons of Italian seasoning
- 2 tablespoons of dried oregano
- 1 pound of okra, well chopped
- Salt to taste

How to Make It:

To prepare soybeans, cover them with water, allowing them to soak overnight.

Combine all the ingredients together in your slow cooker. Use a spoon to mix all the ingredients together until combined.

Cook sauce covered for 12 hours on low. Stir every 3-4 hours.

NOTE: This is a good recipe to start the night before. It can be cooked for up to 24 hours on low without a problem.

Servings:

Makes 12 servings.

∾Spinach and Bean Vegan Enchilada∾

This recipe is a fun take on enchiladas that is completely vegan. These enchiladas are full of delicious veggies like corn, romaine, tomatoes, radishes and more. It makes a delicious dinner and you can always take the leftovers to work for lunch the next day. The enchiladas taste like a gourmet dish, and no one will believe how little time you spent in the kitchen working on this meal.

What You'll Need:

- 2 jars of salsa (16oz)
- 2 tablespoons of olive oil
- 1 can of black beans, well rinsed (15.5 oz)
- 8 corn tortillas (6-inch), warmed
- ½ cucumber, halved and then thinly sliced
- 3 tablespoons of lime juice
- ½ teaspoon of ground cumin
- 10oz package of chopped frozen spinach, thawed and well drained
- ½ cup of grape tomatoes, cut in half
- 1 head of romaine, chopped (about 6 cups)
- 1 cup of frozen corn, thawed
- Black pepper to taste
- Salt to taste
- 4 radishes, finely sliced
- Scallions, finely sliced as a garnish

How to Make It:

Place half of the beans in a medium bowl, mashing them up.

Add the rest of the beans, spinach, cumin, corn, pepper and salt. Stir well until the ingredients are well combined.

In the bottom of your slow cooker, spread one jar of salsa.

Divide the bean mixture among the tortillas, rolling them up and placing them in the slow cooker with the seam side down. Make sure they fit in a single layer. Pour in the rest of the salsa to top the enchiladas.

Cover the slow cooker, cooking on low for about 3 hours.

When almost ready to serve, in a large bowl, toss together the cucumber, romaine, tomatoes and radishes. Add a bit of salt and pepper, the olive oil and the lime juice, tossing again to coat the veggies. Serve the fresh veggies with the warm enchiladas, garnishing with the scallions.

NOTE: You can also top enchiladas with a bit of vegan cheese if desired.

Servings:

Makes 4 servings.

❧Black Bean and Tomatillo Quinoa Vegan Recipe❧

Quinoa is a delicious grain that packs a powerful punch of fiber and protein. This recipe adds tomatillo salsa to the quinoa, along with some other spices that really amp up the flavor in this delicious dish. The black beans add even more protein, so you are sure to be full and satisfied when you finish eating this main dish for dinner. Enjoy garnishing the quinoa with a squeeze of lime, some chopped cilantro and a few diced tomatoes for a beautiful, and tasty, presentation.

What You'll Need:

Quinoa Ingredients

- 1 ½ cups of water
- 1 teaspoon of salt
- 1 can of black beans, thoroughly rinsed and then drained (14 oz)
- ¾ cup of quinoa, uncooked, well rinsed
- 1 teaspoon of cumin
- 1 teaspoon of garlic powder
- 1 bay leaf
- Lime juice, diced tomatoes and chopped cilantro for garnishing

Tomatillo Salsa

- 1 cup of cilantro, coarsely chopped
- 1 teaspoon of kosher salt
- 1 clove of garlic
- ½ pound of tomatillos, rinsed, husked and cut in half
- 2 tablespoons of onion, chopped
- 1 jalapeno, seeds and membrane removed

How to Make It:

Make the tomatillo salsa ahead of time. To make the salsa, place all of your ingredients for the salsa into a food processor or a blender. Pulse a few times to begin chopping up ingredients, then process on high or blend in the blender until you have a salsa consistency. Add a bit more salt to taste if desired.

To make the quinoa mixture, add the quinoa, cumin, black beans, water, salt, bay leaf, garlic powder and prepared tomatillo salsa to your slow cooker.

Cover with the lid and allow to cook on low for 4 hours.

Serve quinoa in bowls while warm, garnishing with the lime juice, cilantro and diced tomato to taste.

Enjoy immediately.

Servings:

Makes 4 servings.

❧Vegan Lentil and Green Chili Slow Cooker Tamales❧

Many people think that it is hard to make tamales, but this recipe makes it easy for you to whip up your own vegan tamales at home without a lot of hard work. It makes a great meal for the weekend, and while it is not difficult to make, it will help to have an extra pair of hands in the kitchen to help you wrap the tamales faster. You will enjoy working with your spouse, kids or a friend while making this tasty, easy tamale slow cooker dish.

What You'll Need:

Filling

- 1 can of lentils, well drained (15 oz)
- 1 can of green chilies (16oz)
- 2 cloves of garlic, chopped finely
- ½ cup of frozen sweet corn, thawed
- ½ onion, diced finely
- 1 tablespoon of olive oil
- ½ teaspoon of cumin
- 1 cube of vegan beef bouillon

Tamale Dough

- 1 teaspoon of salt
- 2 teaspoons of baking powder
- 1 pack of dried corn husks (16 oz)
- 4 cups of masa
- 3 cubes of vegan beef bouillon dissolved in three cups of water
- 1 cup of melted coconut oil

How to Make It:

Place corn husks in a big bowl of warm water, allowing them to soak while you work on the tamale dough and filling.

Meanwhile, heat olive oil in a skillet, adding the garlic and onions, cooking for one minute.

Add the bouillon cube, cumin and lentils, mixing up thoroughly.

Then add corn and green chilies.

Allow to warm up, mix and then remove from heat, setting to the side.

Mix together the salt, baking powder and masa in a large bowl.

Stir melted coconut oil into the dry ingredients.

Add the water with the bouillon to the mixture. If needed, you can add more water to ensure the dough is spongy and soft.

Press bits of masa dough into the biggest corn husks, ensuring that you cover about three square inches of the husk.

Add in a couple tablespoons of the filling, right in the middle of the dough.

Fold up the tamales and place in the slow cooker.

Cover the slow cooker, allowing to cook on high for about 5-6 hours. Tamale dough should be set.

15 minutes before serving, remove the slow cooker lid and unplug the slow cooker.

Allow tamales to sit and cool for about 15 minutes.

Serve tamales while warm.

Servings:

Makes 24 tamales.

Chapter 4: Vegan Slow Cooker Soup and Stew Recipes

The slow cooker is perfect for cooking up delectable soup and stew recipes. It allows soups and stews to cook all day long, which lets you enjoy a delicious, warm meal at the end of the day. From the Mediterranean Vegan Stew to an incredible recipe for vegan Louisiana gumbo, you will enjoy trying out all these incredible soup and stew recipes. They are all easy to whip up in your slow cooker, allowing you to serve up gourmet tasting meals without a lot of work and time in the kitchen.

&Vegan Louisiana Slow Cooker Gumbo&

Most gumbo recipes call for meat in them, but if you are craving the delicious, Louisiana flavors, you can make your own vegan gumbo without a problem. This vegan gumbo recipe adds some other great veggies like okra and tomatoes, giving you a Creole style gumbo that is packed with amazing flavors.

What You'll Need:

- 1 green bell pepper, chopped
- 1 teaspoon of thyme
- 1 tablespoon of olive oil
- ½ teaspoon of salt
- 1 ½ cups of okra, cut in half
- 3 cups of vegetable stock
- 1 teaspoon of filé powder
- 1 onion, chopped
- 1 can of diced tomatoes (14 oz)
- 3 garlic cloves, finely minced
- 3 celery stalks, finely sliced
- 3 cups of water
- 3 cups of pre-cooked rice
- Black pepper to taste
- 1 zucchini, thinly sliced
- Tabasco sauce, to taste

How to Make It:

In a medium sized skillet, heat up the olive oil. Add the bell pepper, garlic, celery and onion, allowing to sauté for a few minutes until tender. Add all the ingredients to the slow cooker, stirring them well until they are all combined. Turn the slow cooker on low, allowing the gumbo to cook for 6-8 hours. Serve gumbo and enjoy while hot.

Servings:

Makes 4-6 servings.

❧Bean, Barley and Veggie Vegan Soup❧

With all the barley and beans, this soup is very filling. This recipe is perfect for a 4-6 quart slow cooker, but if you want to make a bigger batch, you can double the recipe and use an 8-10 quart slow cooker. The leftovers keep really well and they are wonderful for lunches during the week as well.

What You'll Need:

- 4 cups of liquid total (including barely soaking liquid and extra water)
- 1 ½ cups of garbanzo beans drained and rinsed (16 oz can)
- ½ cup of pearl barley, soaked for at least 4 hours
- 1 ½ cups of kidney beans (16 oz can), rinsed and well drained
- 2 medium carrots, peeled and chopped
- 2 tablespoons of olive oil
- ½ pound of green beans, cut into 1 inch pieces
- 2 cloves of garlic, minced
- 2 stalks of celery, diced
- 3 potatoes, peeled and chopped
- 1 teaspoon each of marjoram, basil, paprika and thyme
- Pinch of cayenne pepper
- ½ red bell pepper, diced
- ½ green bell pepper, diced
- ½ teaspoon of ground fennel
- 1 vegetable bouillon cube
- 1 tablespoon of Bragg's Liquid Aminos
- 2 thin fresh ginger slices, minced
- 1 bay leaf
- 3 tablespoons of tomato paste
- Salt to taste
- 2 tablespoons of fresh parsley, minced

How to Make It:

Cook pearl barley after it soaks in water for at least four hours. Keep the soaking water to go into the soup with the barley.

Add all the ingredients to the slow cooker, except for the fresh herbs, cayenne pepper, salt and Bragg's Liquid Aminos.

Cover and allow to cook on low for about six hours.

Remove lid and add Bragg's Liquid Aminos, fresh herbs, cayenne pepper and salt.

Allow to cook for 15 more minutes.

Serve soup in bowls, eating while warm.

NOTE: You can choose to sauté veggies before adding to the slow cooker if you desire. This will make the soup cook quicker. To cook faster in a slow cooker, sauté spices and veggies, add ingredients to slow cooker and cook on high for three hours.

Servings:

Makes 4 servings.

❧Mediterranean Vegan Stew❧

Not only is this Mediterranean vegan stew full of flavor, but it is so easy to make. In fact, it barely takes any prep time in the kitchen at all. You will get plenty of nutrition from all the veggies, including eggplant, squash, tomato, carrots, onions and more. It is perfect on a cool evening, but it is just as delicious during the summer for a light evening meal. The cinnamon and raisins add an interesting flavor that provides a bit of sweetness with the rest of the vegetables used in this recipe.

What You'll Need:

- 1 cup of onion, chopped
- ½ cup of raisins
- ¼ teaspoon of crushed red pepper
- 1 butternut squash, peeled, seeds removed and cut into cubes
- 1 ripe tomato, roughly chopped
- ½ cup of vegetable broth
- ¼ teaspoon of ground cinnamon
- 2 cups of eggplant, cubed with the skin left on
- ½ teaspoon of ground turmeric
- ¼ teaspoon of paprika
- 1 clove of garlic, finely chopped
- 1 can of tomato sauce (8oz)
- 2 cups of zucchini, cubed
- ½ teaspoon of ground cumin
- 1 pack of frozen okra (10 oz) thawed completely
- 1 carrot, thinly sliced

How to Make It:

Combine all the ingredients together in a slow cooker. Stir well to make sure the seasonings are mixed throughout.

Place the lid on the slow cooker, cooking for 8-10 hours on low, ensuring that vegetables become tender before serving.

Serve in soup bowls while hot and enjoy.

Servings:

Makes 10 servings.

Pasta Kidney Bean Vegan Soup

This is another delicious soup recipe that does not take a lot of work on your part. It includes great protein from the beans and the pasta really adds to the finished soup. Make sure you use whole wheat pasta to get even more nutritional benefits in the soup. It uses a lot of veggies, and if you do not have a couple of the veggies on hand, you can substitute in any that you do. You will still end up with a delicious soup that is wonderful for lunch or dinner.

What You'll Need:

- 1 tablespoon of olive oil
- 1 cup of fresh green beans, sliced
- 1 cup of whole wheat penne pasta dry (cook to al dente, rinse with some cold water, then sit to the side)
- 1 teaspoon of dried basil
- 1 cup of kidney beans (canned), drained and then rinsed
- 1 potato, peeled and cut into cubes
- ¼ cup of onion, diced
- 1 teaspoon of dried marjoram
- 2 celery stalks, thinly sliced
- 1 jalapeno pepper, finely minced
- 2 cloves of garlic, finely minced
- 1 carrot, peeled and thinly sliced
- ½ teaspoon of thyme
- ½ teaspoon of salt
- 1/8 teaspoon of cayenne pepper
- ½ red bell pepper, chopped
- ½ teaspoon of oregano
- ½ teaspoon of cumin
- 1 cup of tomato sauce
- 4 cups of vegetable stock
- 1 teaspoon of coriander, ground
- ¼ cup of fresh parsley, chopped

How to Make It:

Boil the pasta until it is al dente, then drain. Carefully rinse with some cold water and set it to the side.

Quickly sauté the jalapeno, onions and garlic until tender and then add to the slow cooker.

Add the rest of the ingredients to the slow cooker, except the green beans, pasta and the chopped parsley.

Cover the slow cooker, allowing the soup to simmer for 4-6 hours on low.

The rest of the veggies should be tender when the soup is done.

Keep the pasta refrigerated while the soup is cooking.

Once veggies are finally tender, add the green beans, pasta and some salt to taste.

Cook for 20-30 more minutes on high heat until the beans and pasta are heated throughout.

Serve the soup in soup bowls, topping with some freshly chopped parsley.

Enjoy immediately while hot.

Servings:

Makes 6 servings.

❧Sweet Potato and Lentil Vegan Soup❧

This delicious soup combines together some amazing Mediterranean flavors. You can serve the soup with some crusty artisan bread or you can top with couscous or rice to make the meal even heartier. You definitely will be filled up after eating a serving of this delicious soup.

What You'll Need:

- 1 tablespoon of minced jalapeno pepper
- ½ cup of red pepper, diced
- 1 tablespoon of olive oil
- 6 cups of vegetable stock
- 1 tablespoon of garlic, finely minced
- ½ cup of green pepper, diced
- 1 teaspoon of coriander, ground
- 3 tablespoons of tomato paste
- 1 cup of brown lentils
- ½ teaspoon of dried thyme
- 1 cup of celery, diced
- Pepper to taste
- ½ teaspoon of cumin, ground
- 1 teaspoon of basil
- 3 cups of sweet potatoes, peeled and cut into cubes
- ¼ cup of fresh parsley, minced
- 1 teaspoon of light molasses
- Dash of Bragg's Liquid Aminos

How to Make It:

In a small skillet, heat up the oil, adding the garlic and sautéing until it is fragrant.

Add all of the ingredients to the cold slow cooker except for the molasses, Bragg's Liquid Aminos and parsley.

Turn to low heat and cook while covered for about 6 hours.

About 20 minutes before serving, add the molasses and Bragg's Liquid Aminos.

Serve the soup hot, topping with some minced fresh parsley.

Servings:

Makes 6 servings.

❧Bean and Quinoa Slow Cooker Vegan Chili❧

Delicious, healthy quinoa is added to black beans, which means you will get plenty of protein when you make this soup, making it perfect for a nice dinner or a lunch. This delicious vegan chili is so tasty that you probably will not have to worry about leftovers.

What You'll Need:

- 1 ½ cup of canned black beans, rinsed and drained
- 1 ½ cup of quinoa, uncooked
- 1 ½ cup of canned kidney beans, rinsed and drained
- 3 cups of water
- 1 stalk of celery, diced
- 1 cup of tomato sauce, unsalted
- ¼ cup of onion, chopped
- 1 tablespoon of olive oil
- ½ red pepper, chopped
- ½ green bell pepper, chopped
- 1 tablespoon of garlic, minced
- 2 tablespoons of jalapeno pepper, minced
- ¼ cup of cilantro, chopped
- 1 tablespoon of Bragg's Liquid Aminos
- 1 tablespoon of molasses
- Ground black pepper, to taste
- Salt, to taste

Herbs and Spices
- 1 teaspoon of basil leaf, dried
- 1 teaspoon of cumin
- 1 teaspoon of paprika
- 2 teaspoons of coriander, ground
- 1 bay leaf
- ½ teaspoon of thyme
- ¼ teaspoon of chipotle pepper powder
- ½ teaspoon of marjoram

How to Make It:

In a medium skillet, sauté the peppers, celery, jalapeno, onions and garlic in the olive oil for about five minutes over medium high heat.

Add herbs and spices, stirring and cooking for another two minutes.

In a slow cooker, combine the tomato sauce, black beans and kidney beans, quinoa, salt, black pepper and water, then add in the vegetable and herb mixture, stirring well to combine.

Cover with the lid, cooking for 5-6 hours on low.

Serve while hot, garnishing with chopped fresh cilantro.

Servings:

Makes 6 servings.

❧Cauliflower Curry Vegan Soup❧

The delicious goodness of cauliflower and the taste tempting flavors of curry powder are mixed together in this recipe, combining to make a delicious soup that is warm and comforting. This soup is perfect for lunch, but you can also make it for a light dinner as well. It is full of other veggies, including celery and carrots, and you can have fun with toppings, topping the soup with cashew cream, walnuts, pepitas, or even some thin slices of apple. If you have leftovers, you can easily freeze them, pulling the leftovers out later for a quick meal when you are in a hurry. This soup comes together in no time and you can start your slow cooker and walk away, coming back for a great meal later when the soup is done cooking.

What You'll Need:

-   1 onion, diced
-   1 head of cauliflower, chopped into small florets
-   1 tablespoon of olive oil
-   1 quart of vegetable stock
-   2 stalks of celery, diced
-   1 bay leaf
-   3 cloves of garlic, minced
-   3 tablespoons of curry powder (you can use paste if you do not have the powder)
-   4 tablespoons of nutritional yeast
-   Fresh pepper, to taste
-   Salt, to taste
-   1 cup of carrots, shredded

How to Make It:

In a skillet, heat the olive oil on medium heat.

Place the celery, garlic, carrots and onion in the hot oil, sautéing for 8-10 minutes until fragrant and tender.

In a slow cooker, combine all the ingredients. Use a wooden spoon to toss the ingredients, mixing until well combined.

50

Cover and cook on low for about four hours or until the vegetables are very soft.

When done cooking, use an immersion blender to blend up the soup until the cauliflower is blended and the soup is creamy.

Add the nutritional yeast to help thicken the soup and blend a bit more.

Taste the soup, adding a bit of salt and pepper to taste.

Serve the soup while warm and enjoy.

Servings:

Makes 4 servings.

Chapter 5: Vegan Slow Cooker Side Dish Recipes

Even tasty side dishes can be easily cooked up in your slow cooker. The wonderful thing about using your slow cooker for side dishes is that you leave your stove or oven available for making the main dish. Slow cooker sides are easy to make and you can easily take them to a pot luck or to a friend's house for a dinner with friends. The vegan marinated mushrooms are sure to please, and the vegan refried beans will go with any Mexican meal you cook up.

❧Vegan Scalloped Potato Slow Cooker Recipe❧

These vegan scalloped potatoes are tasty, especially with the flavor of the cashews in them. They come together in no time at all. In just 10-15 minutes, you will have all the prep done, then the slow cooker will do the rest. Enjoy along with a delicious dinner. Your family will definitely want you to make this recipe again.

What You'll Need:

-   6 large russet potatoes
-   1 cup of organic, raw cashews
-   ¾ teaspoon of garlic powder
-   ¾ teaspoon of sea salt
-   1 ½ cups of soy milk
-   1 cup of nutritional yeast

How to Make It:

Peel the potatoes and then slice them very thinly.

Combine the cashews, sea salt, garlic powder, soy milk and the nutritional yeast together in a food processor. Process until you have a creamy, smooth sauce.

Place 1/3 of the potatoes in the slow cooker, then top with about 1/3 of the creamy sauce.

Repeat with the rest of the potatoes and sauce, layering and ending with the sauce.

Cover and set heat on low, allowing to cook for 6-8 hours.

Serve immediately while the potatoes are hot.

Servings:

Makes 8 servings.

❧Tasty Vegan Marinated Mushrooms❧

Mushrooms are delicious and have very few calories, which makes them a delicious side dish if you are counting calories and working to eat healthy. These easy to make marinated mushrooms have all the flavor that comes from some vegan butter, a bit of sugar and some Bragg's Liquid Aminos. Make sure you make up plenty of these mushrooms, because they are sure to be a big hit when you serve them.

What You'll Need:

- 32 ounces of fresh button mushrooms, stems removed
- 2 cups of Bragg's Liquid Aminos
- 1 cup of vegan butter
- 2 cups of sugar (or sugar substitute)
- 2 cups of water

How to Make It:

Mix together the vegan butter, Bragg's Liquid Aminos and water in a medium size saucepan.

Heat on low, continuing to stir until the vegan butter is fully melted.

Add the sugar or substitute gradually, allowing to cook on low until it dissolves.

Place all the mushrooms into a slow cooker prepared with cooking spray.

Pour the sugar mixture over the mushrooms.

Cover the slow cooker and set to low heat.

Allow to cook for 8-10 hours, taking time to stir the mushrooms every hour or two.

Serve warm or chill and serve cold, depending on your preference.

Servings:

Makes 8-16 servings (depending on serving sizes).

Maple Bourbon Vegan Baked Beans

If you are looking for a fabulous vegan baked bean recipe, your search is over. This recipe is so easy and it creates the most delicious baked beans. While it takes time to cook, it will not take much time out of your day, since the slow cooker is doing all the hard work for you. You are sure to appreciate the combination of flavors, including molasses, maple syrup, bourbon, brown sugar and tangy BBQ sauce. As they cook the flavors combine and provide you with a smooth, delicious sauce for the baked beans.

What You'll Need:

- 1 cup of barbeque sauce (your favorite)
- 1 cup of bourbon
- 1 pound of Great Northern beans, dry
- 1 cup of light brown sugar, packed
- 1 cup of maple syrup
- ¼ cup of yellow mustard
- 14 cups of water
- ¼ cup of olive oil
- ¼ cup of ketchup, heaping
- ¼ cup of apple cider vinegar
- 2 tablespoons of Bragg's Liquid Aminos
- ¼ cup of light molasses

How to Make It:

Carefully rinse beans in a colander, sorting as you rinse.

Place beans in a large pot, covering them with about eight cups of water.

Allow to soak for 8 hours or follow the rapid soak method found on the package of beans.

After beans are ready, drain in a colander, rinsing the beans well before using them.

Place beans in a pot, add six cups of water and turn burner on low, allowing beans to simmer for 45-50 minutes or until they are tender.

They should be about 80% cooked. They do not need to be completely done, since they will be cooking for a long time in the slow cooker.

As beans simmer, place the rest of the ingredients in your slow cooker, whisking together until well combined and smooth.

Drain the beans and then pour them into the slow cooker, stirring well to coat all the beans.

Cover the slow cooker, turning on low heat and cooking them for about 12 hours.

Beans should be very tender and you should have a reduced, thick sauce that tastes delicious.

If the liquid has not thickened up enough, increase heat to high, take off the lid and cook uncovered until the sauce thickens up.

Serve the beans while hot. Leftover beans can be placed in an airtight container and refrigerated for up to 7 days.

Servings:

Makes 8 1-cup servings.

❧Rice and Mushroom Vegan Side Dish❧

Are you looking for a side dish that is quick and easy? If so, you will definitely love this rice and mushroom vegan recipe. This recipe is family friendly, and you can be sure that everyone will enjoy this delicious dish. To make the flavor a bit milder, you can use regular mushroom soup instead of portabella mushroom soup, ensuring that you choose vegan mushroom soup. This is not only a great side dish, but it is filling enough that you may want to make it the main course for dinner.

What You'll Need:

- 2 teaspoons of salt
- 1 box of portabella soup (32 oz)
- 1 bag of long grain rice (16 oz)
- ¼ teaspoon of black pepper
- 2 medium onions, diced
- 8 ounces of white button mushrooms, sliced
- ½ cup of vegan butter, melted

How to Make It:

Place the soup, rice, onion, pepper, salt and melted vegan butter to the slow cooker.

Lay all the sliced mushrooms on top of the rest of the ingredients, pushing them into the liquid, keeping the rice beneath the liquid so it softens and ensuring that the mushrooms cook a little slower than the rest of the ingredients.

Cover and cook on low for about 6-8 hours.

When done cooking, uncover the slow cooker, using a fork to fluff up the rice, stirring the mushrooms into the rice.

Serve while hot and enjoy.

Servings:

Makes 6 servings.

❧Slow Cooker Vegan Refried Beans❧

Forget buying refried beans in a can. This recipe allows you to make your own vegan refried beans that make a tasty addition to any Mexican themed meal. The great thing is that you can whip up these vegan refried beans without a whole lot of work, making your slow cooker take care of all the preparation.

What You'll Need:

- 1 small onion, diced finely
- 1 bag of pinto beans (1 lb)
- 1 chile pepper, diced finely
- ½ teaspoon of oregano
- 2 tablespoons of olive oil
- 1 teaspoon of salt
- 4 cloves of garlic, diced finely
- 1 teaspoon of cumin
- ½ teaspoon of chili powder
- 6-8 cups of water

How to Make It:

The night before, sort and rinse the beans and allow them to drain.

In a large pot, add six cups of water, ensuring that the water covers the pinto beans.

Let the pot of beans sit overnight, allowing the beans to plump up.

Drain the beans and then place them into the slow cooker.

Add water to the slow cooker, covering the beans with about 1-2 inches of water.

Cook beans on high for about three hours. As the beans cook, begin preparing the veggies.

Heat the olive oil in a large skillet, adding the onion and sautéing until the onion is tender and translucent.

Add chili pepper and garlic, allowing to cook for 2-3 more minutes.

Place the oregano, cumin and chili powder in the skillet, cooking for another minute while stirring. Set veggie mixture to the side.

Once beans are done cooking, use a potato masher to mash them while still in the slow cooker.

Add the vegetables to the slow cooker, mixing together with the mashed beans. Add a little water if the mixture seems too dry.

Turn the slow cooker to low, cooking the beans for another hour.

Serve the beans while hot and enjoy.

Store leftovers in the refrigerator for up to a week.

Servings:

Makes 10 servings.

❧Vegan Apple and Sweet Potato❧

The sweet goodness of sweet potatoes and apples are combined in this delightful side dish. It is easy to make and will not require a lot of preparation time. The cinnamon spiced syrup really adds something special to this side dish.

What You'll Need:

- 4 small red apples (Choose your favorite)
- ¼ cup of apple juice + 2 tablespoons of apple juice, divided
- 3 large sweet potatoes
- 1 teaspoon of cinnamon
- 1 teaspoon of cornstarch
- Dash of nutmeg to taste
- 2 tablespoons of brown sugar (or more to taste)

How to Make It:

Wash and peel the apples and the sweet potatoes, chopping them into 1 inch pieces.

Place the pieces of apple and sweet potato in your slow cooker.

In a small bowl, stir together the nutmeg, brown sugar, ¼ cup of apple juice and the cinnamon, combining with a whisk.

Pour the cinnamon mixture over the sweet potatoes and apples, then stir well to make sure everything is well coated.

Turn heat to high, cooking for about 3 hours.

In a small measuring cup, stir 2 tablespoons of apple juice together with a teaspoon of cornstarch.

Remove the cover of the slow cooker, slowing stirring in the cornstarch mixture to thicken the sauce.

Allow to cook for a few more minutes or until the sauce thickens.

Serve while hot and enjoy the delicious combination of flavors.

Servings:

Makes 8 servings.

Chapter 6: Vegan Slow Cooker Casserole Recipes

Sometimes it is just nice to have a good casserole for dinner. With these one pot recipes you will not have to worry about cooking anything else to serve alongside the casserole. If you love southwestern flavors, you will definitely want to give the Southwestern Vegan Casserole a try. For curry lovers, the Curried Lentil and Rice Vegan Casserole is sure to be a huge hit. The best thing about these one pot casseroles is that they are so easy to make, making dinner easier and faster than ever.

❧One-Pot Southwestern Vegan Casserole❧

This easy casserole allows you to create a one pot dinner and it will not take much time to get everything ready to start cooking. While the recipe calls for black eyed peas, you can substitute in any beans that you may have around instead if you do not have the black eyed peas on hand. Use canned beans if you have them so you do not have to waste time worrying about soaking the beans or peas.

What You'll Need:

- 1 green bell pepper, chopped
- 2 teaspoons of cumin, ground
- 1 ½ cup of canned black eyed peas (or other beans)
- ¼ cup of chili powder
- 1 can of sweet corn, well drained (10 oz)
- 2 cups of cooked rice (brown or other rice)
- 1 can of diced tomatoes (28 oz)
- 1 onion, diced
- 2 cloves of garlic, minced
- Vegan shredded cheese (optional)

How to Make It:

Make sure that the black eyed peas are drained and rinsed.

Add the peas, peppers, tomatoes, corn, garlic, onion, cumin and chili powder in the slow cooker.

Stir well to make sure ingredients are thoroughly blended together.

Cover the slow cooker, allowing to cook on high for about two hours.

After two hours, stir in the cooked rice.

Cook for 30-40 more minutes until all the flavors combine.

Serve on plates, topping with vegan shredded cheese if desired. Enjoy.

Servings:

Makes 6 servings.

❧Mushroom and Tempeh Stroganoff Vegan Casserole❧

When you cook up this tasty casserole, you will enjoy many delicious flavors, even though it uses only a few ingredients. The sauce is made from the bouillon and the mushrooms, providing a rich flavor to the dish. While some people think that Tempeh has a bit of a bitter taste, you can eliminate that taste by steaming it for 8-10 minutes before placing it in your slow cooker. Not only is this recipe vegan, but you can make it gluten free by using gluten free pasta. It is so delicious that you may want to double this recipe so you have enough for the whole family.

What You'll Need:

- 2 cups of chopped button mushrooms
- 1 teaspoon of vegan "chicken" bouillon
- 1/3 cup of vegan sour cream (or you can use non-dairy milk or cashew cream)
- 2 cloves of garlic, chopped finely
- 1 package of tempeh (8 oz)
- Pinch of dill
- 1-2 cups of water (you may need more if you cook the casserole over 8 hours)
- ½ teaspoon of paprika
- Pepper to taste
- Salt to taste
- Cooked pasta of choice, for serving

How to Make It:

The night before you want to make this recipe, chop up the mushrooms and the tempeh.

Steam your tempeh for 8-10 minutes to take away any bitter taste.

Store tempeh and mushrooms in the refrigerator until you are ready to prepare the recipe the next day.

In the morning, place the paprika, bouillon, garlic, mushrooms, water and tempeh to the slow cooker, turning on low and cooking for 7-9 hours.

About 20 minutes before you plan to serve the stroganoff, add the vegan sour cream to the slow cooker, mixing it well with the rest of ingredients.

Add some pepper and salt to taste, adding just a bit more paprika if you desire.

Serve hot over pasta and garnish with a bit of dill. You can also serve this stroganoff over quinoa or rice for a different taste.

Servings:

Makes 2-3 servings.

☙Tasty Mexicali Vegan Rice Casserole❧

When you eat this casserole, you will enjoy a delicious blend of California and Mexican flavors, giving the dish its name, "Mexicali." With all the veggies, the black beans and the rice, you have a filling casserole that is packed with nutritious goodness. The lime juice, orange juice, cilantro and chili powder combine to provide plenty of delicious flavors that will make your taste buds sing with joy when you taste this vegan casserole. You may want to make extra so you can take leftovers to work for lunch the next day. If you are feeding a bunch, you may want to double the recipe. It is a great recipe to take with you to a potluck or to a big dinner with friends and family members.

What You'll Need:

- 4 ounces of green chilies, diced
- 1 can of corn, drained (15 oz)
- 1 red bell pepper, diced
- 1 can of black beans, rinsed and drained (15 oz)
- 1 large onion, diced
- ½ cup of orange juice concentrate, thawed
- 2 cups of long grain rice, uncooked
- 3 ½ cups of boiling water
- 1 ½ tablespoons of cumin, ground
- 4 ½ tablespoons of lime juice, fresh and divided
- 1/3 cup of fresh, chopped cilantro
- 1 tablespoon of chili powder
- 1 teaspoon of fresh ground black pepper
- 1 teaspoon of salt

How to Make It:

Prepare a slow cooker with cooking spray or use a slow cooker liner.

Combine together the bell pepper, onion, corn, chilies, black beans, orange juice, rice, water, ¼ cup of the lime juice, chili powder and cumin in the slow cooker.

Stir well ensuring that the ingredients are combined thoroughly.

Cover the slow cooker and turn the heat on low.

Allow to cook on low for about 2 ½ hours, ensuring that veggies are tender and the rice is cooked. Cook a bit longer if necessary.

Stir in the salt, pepper, cilantro and the rest of the lime juice when the casserole is done cooking.

Make sure to stir well to spread out the flavors throughout.

Serve immediately while the casserole is hot.

Servings:

Makes 4-6 servings.

❧Curried Lentil and Rice Vegan Casserole❧

This tasty curried lentil and rice casserole has its roots in traditional Indian dishes. The curry is delicious and adds plenty of flavor to the lentils and rice. While this is a delightful casserole dish that will fill you up, you can reduce the servings and serve this as a side dish as well if you desire. The garlic and onion compliments the curry powder well, and once you taste this casserole, you will definitely want to make it again and again.

What You'll Need:

- 3 ½ cups of vegetable stock or broth
- 1 cup of rice (brown, white or basmati)
- 1 onion, finely diced
- 1 tablespoon of curry powder
- ½ teaspoon of garlic powder
- ½ cup of lentils
- ¼ teaspoon of pepper
- 2 vegan bouillon cubes

How to Make It:

In a slow cooker, combine all the ingredients. Stir them together.

Cover the slow cooker, turning the heat on low and allowing to cook for 4-5 hours.

When finished cooking, serve immediate while hot and enjoy.

Leftovers can be refrigerated for 2-3 days and reheated in the microwave.

Servings:

Makes 4 servings. (NOTE: Makes 8 servings if using it as a side dish)

Chapter 7: Vegan Slow Cooker Dessert Recipes

Yes, you can even fix dessert in your slow cooker. These vegan desserts are all quite simple to make and you can throw the ingredients in your slow cooker and walk away. When the cooking is done, you will have a tasty dessert that tastes like you spent hours in the kitchen. The best part is that your slow cooker is doing all the work for you. Try the baked apples after a big dinner or wow guests with the amazing Vegan Chocolate Chip Slow Cooker Bread Pudding. Every dessert is sure to please, and you are sure to make these dessert recipes again and again.

❧Blueberry Vegan Rice Pudding❧

This rice pudding recipe is totally vegan and it uses rice milk instead of regular milk. You only need a bit of sugar to sweeten the dessert and the cinnamon and nutmeg just add to the delicious flavors. Make sure you serve this while it is warm, since it tastes the best while warm and gooey. The best part about this recipe is that it makes a lot, so it is easy to serve your family and guests.

What You'll Need:

- ½ cup of organic sugar
- ½ bag of frozen blueberries, thawed
- 3 cups of long grain white rice, uncooked
- 32 oz of vanilla rice milk
- 4 tablespoons of vegan margarine
- Cinnamon to taste
- Nutmeg to taste
- Extra blueberry syrup for serving (optional)

How to Make It:

In the microwave or on the stove top, cook the long grain rice, following the instructions on the package.

Add the rice milk and the cooked rice to a slow cooker that has been sprayed with nonstick cooking spray.

Stir the milk and rice together until well combined.

Add the thawed blueberries, the sugar, margarine and the cinnamon and nutmeg to taste.

Cover the mixture, turning heat to low and allowing to cook for three hours. Stir every hour.

After the pudding becomes thick, you are ready to serve.

Serve in dessert dishes, topping with a bit of blueberry syrup if desired. Top with a dash of cinnamon.

Serve while warm and enjoy right away.

Servings:

Makes 15 servings.

❧Slow Cooker Baked Apple Vegan Dessert❧

Not only is this vegan apple dessert delicious, but it is actually a healthy dessert choice as well. It tastes like a piece of apple pie, but it is so much better for you since you do not have the fat laden crust. You will love how easy this recipe is to put together and once you have it in the slow cooker, you can forget about it until you are ready to serve it. Get the kids involved to let them help you cook this dessert, since it is easy enough for them to help with it. The best part is that this dish will make your house smell amazing as it is cooking, which makes it a great dessert to serve if you have company coming over for dinner.

What You'll Need:

- 6 Macintosh or Gala apples, cored
- ¼ cup of brown sugar, packed
- ½ cup of apple cider
- ¼ cup of chopped walnuts
- 1 teaspoon of cinnamon
- 2 tablespoons of vegan butter or margarine
- 2 tablespoons of orange liquor (optional)

How to Make It:

Mix together the vegan margarine or butter, brown sugar, cinnamon and the walnuts, stirring well. (NOTE: You can use pecans instead of the walnuts if you desire)

Carefully core the apples, just leaving a bit of apple on the bottom so it sits on the bottom of the slow cooker without tipping. It also keeps the apple from falling apart as it cooks in the slow cooker.

Place the six apples in the slow cooker, filling each apple with some of the brown sugar filling.

In a small bowl, mix together the apple cider and the liquor if you are using it. Mix well and the pour it over and around the apples.

Cover the apples and turn the slow cooker on high, cooking the apples for 3 hours.

Apples should be very soft when they are done.

Serve the apples while they are hot.

Leftovers can be refrigerated for 2-3 days as long as they are stored in an airtight container.

Servings:

Makes 6 servings.

❧Delicious Vegan Chocolate Chip Slow Cooker Bread Pudding❧

Whether you are throwing a dinner party or you just want a delectable dessert to enjoy on a Sunday night, you are sure to enjoy this delicious chocolate chip slow cooker bread pudding. You will enjoy the combined flavors of apple brandy, apples, chopped nuts and vegan chocolate chips. No one will ever guess that this is a vegan recipe, even if you have friends that are not eating a vegan diet.

What You'll Need:

- 4 tablespoons of apple brandy
- 4 cups of cubed whole wheat bread, stale (gluten free if desired)
- ½ cup of vegan chocolate chips
- 3 cups of peeled and minced apples
- 2 tablespoons of ground flaxseeds, mixed together with 4 tablespoons of warm water
- 2/3 cup of chopped pecans or walnuts
- 1-2 cups of nondairy milk
- ½ cup of sugar, sugar substitute or other sweetener (to taste)

How to Make It:

Spray the slow cooker with some nonstick cooking spray or you can use a slow cooker liner, since this recipe can be a bit messy.

In a large bowl, combine the apples, bread, 1 cup of the milk, flaxseed mixture, brandy and the sweetener.

Mix well and allow to soak for 10-15 minutes, ensuring the bread soaks up the liquid.

If the mixture seems too dry, you can add another cup of milk.

Add the chocolate and the nuts to the bowl and mix well.

Use a spoon to transfer the mixture into your slow cooker.

Cover and then turn slow cooker to high.

Cook for 1.5 to 2 hours.

Serve the bread pudding while it is warm and enjoy immediately.

Servings:

Makes 8 servings.

❧Slow Cooker Vegan Kheer Dessert❧

This is an Indian inspired dessert that is much like rice pudding. It gets flavored with raisins, nuts and some cardamom, making a fabulous, creamy dessert that you will really enjoy. The brown rice used in this recipe makes it more nutritious than most rice pudding recipes. Not only does it taste wonderful for dessert, but leftovers make a great breakfast as well. You can easily make this dessert without needing to spend a whole lot of time slaving away in the kitchen.

What You'll Need:

- 6 cups of nondairy milk (coconut, almond or soy milk all work fine)
- 1 teaspoon of cardamom
- 1 cup of long grain brown rice, cooked
- ½ cup of golden raisins
- 2 tablespoons of agave nectar
- 2 tablespoons of sugar (or sugar substitute)
- ½ cup of slivered almonds

How to Make It:

Combine all the ingredients in the slow cooker, except for the agave nectar and the sugar. Mix together the ingredients until they are well incorporated.

Cover the slow cooker, turning the heat on low and allowing to cook for 4-5 hours.

Once the pudding is thick and fully cooked, add the sugar and the agave nectar to the pudding, mixing well to thoroughly distribute the sweeteners throughout.

Taste the pudding and add a bit more sweetener to taste if you desire.

Allow the pudding to cool, placing the pudding in a large serving bowl.

Cover and put in the refrigerator for a few hours to chill. It thickens as it cools in the refrigerator.

Serve the pudding cold, topping it with more nuts and raisins if desired.

Enjoy the delicious combinations of flavors.

Servings:

Makes 8 servings.

❧Slow Cooker Creamsicle Vegan Tapioca Dessert❧

If you are looking for a cool, refreshing dessert for the warm summer months, this slow cooker recipe is the perfect option. You can make this cool dessert without having to use your oven, so you will not heat up your home trying to make it. The orange extract used in the tapioca makes it taste like a delicious orange creamsicle, something that will bring back memories of your childhood. Even better, each serving has less than 80 calories, which means this is a guilt free dessert that you can enjoy, knowing that it is good for you. This is so delicious that you may want to double the recipe to make sure you have plenty around so you can have a second helping later.

What You'll Need:

- 1 teaspoon of vanilla
- 4 cups of vanilla coconut milk (sugar free)
- ½ cup of small pearl tapioca
- 2 teaspoons of orange extract
- Sugar for extra sweetening, if needed

How to Make It:

This recipe is for a 3-4 quart slow cooker, so you may need to double the recipe for larger slow cookers for the best results.

Mix together all the ingredients in the slow cooker.

After combining the ingredients until well mixed, cover and cook for 3.5 to 4.5 hours on low heat. To speed it up, you can cook on high for 2 hours instead.

Once the tapioca is done cooking, taste it to see if you need to add a bit of extra sweetener to it. It may seem a bit runny, but it will set in the refrigerator, so do not worry about it.

Place the tapioca in a serving bowl and allow to cool. When mostly cool, cover it and place it in the refrigerator so it can set.

After it has totally cooled, then you can serve chilled, enjoying right away for a delicious, cool treat that you are sure to appreciate on a warm evening.

Servings:

Makes 6 servings.

Vegan Slow Cooker Pumpkin Pudding Dessert

You are going to love this pudding recipe because it is just so easy and it makes a pudding that is just as delicious as a sweet, pumpkin pie. It only requires about 10-15 minutes of prep time and then you can allow the slow cooker to take care of the rest. If you serve this dessert to guests, they are definitely going to want the recipe.

What You'll Need:

- ½ cup of flour
- 1 can of solid pack pumpkin (15 oz)
- ¼ teaspoon of salt
- 2 teaspoons of pumpkin pie spice
- 12 ounces of soy, almond or coconut milk
- 2 tablespoons of sugar substitute, like Splenda or Stevia
- ¾ cup of brown sugar (or brown sugar substitute)
- ½ cup of egg substitute
- 2 tablespoons of vegan butter or margarine
- ½ teaspoon of baking powder

How to Make It:

Place pumpkin in a large bowl, using a spoon to beat it, softening the pumpkin.

Add in ¼ of the vegan milk gradually, using a whisk to blend it together with pumpkin.

Add the rest of the milk and all the ingredients, except the brown sugar.

Beat with a hand mixer until the ingredients are well blended.

Coat a slow cooker with nonstick cooking spray.

Put the pumpkin mixture into the slow cooker.

Cover the slow cooker, turning the heat on low and allowing the pudding to cook for 5-7 hours.

The pudding should set when it is done.

Pudding can be served warm or you can chill the pudding for a cool, pumpkin treat. If you want to serve the pudding cool, make sure you place it in an airtight container and refrigerate for several hours to ensure it is completely cool.

Servings:

Makes 6-8 servings.

❧Tasty Vegan Applesauce❧

If you want a healthy, delicious dessert, then this applesauce recipe is sure to please. It is easy to put the ingredients together, cooking in the slow cooker while you worry about the rest of your meal. When you are ready for dessert, the applesauce will be done and ready for you to enjoy. This recipe is so easy that your kids could easily make it. In fact, you may want to let your kids mix up this delicious applesauce recipe so they can brag about their great dessert.

What You'll Need:

- ½ teaspoon of pumpkin pie spice
- 8 apples (any kind), peeled, cored and sliced thinly
- ¾ cup of brown sugar, packed
- ½ cup of water

How to Make It:

Spray a slow cooker with some nonstick cooking spray.

Combine the water and apples in the prepared slow cooker.

Turn heat to low, cooking the apples for 6-8 hours.

After apples become very tender, stir in the pumpkin pie spice and the brown sugar.

Cover again and allow the apples to cook for 30-40 more minutes.

Use a potato masher to mash the apples into a sauce.

Serve warm and enjoy.

Servings:

Makes 8 servings.

❧Vegan Sugar-Free Peach Cobbler❧

It is hard to believe that this peach cobbler is sugar free and vegan, it just tastes so wonderful when you make it. Whether someone in your house has diabetes or you are trying to cut back on sugar, this dessert is sure to please. The great part is that you can throw this recipe together in no time and allow it to cook so it is ready to enjoy after dinner. While the recipe calls for fresh peaches, you can always try it with other fruit, such as apples or pears, for a nice change.

What You'll Need:

- 2/3 cup of rolled oats
- ½ cup of brown sweetener
- ½ cup of white sweetener
- 4 cups of fresh peaches, thinly sliced
- 1/3 cup of Bisquick
- ¼ teaspoon of ground cinnamon

How to Make It:

Carefully spray the entire slow cooker with some nonstick cooking spray before adding ingredients.

In a large bowl, mix together the rolled oats, brown sugar, sugar, Bisquick and the cinnamon. Mix well until combined.

Stir the fresh peaches into the mix, combining well. Pour the peach mixture into your slow cooker.

Cover the peach cobbler, cooking for 4-6 hours on low heat.

When the peaches are tender and the mixture is bubbling, it is done.

Serve up the peach cobbler while it is warm, enjoying the fruity goodness right away.

Servings:

Makes 4-6 servings.

Free Bonus

Right after I wrote this book, I wrote another slow cooker cookbook called "The Paleo Slow Cooker Cookbook". Many of the recipes included in this new book, whilst being paleo, are also vegan. As such I thought I would give away three of these recipes as a thank you for purchasing this book.

The recipes are as follows:

- Sweet Potato and Apple Slow Cooker Breakfast Spread
- Cinnamon and Apple Cider Butternut Squash Soup
- Stuffed Apple Slow Cooker Recipe

I love these recipes as they all contain my favorite fruit – the apple.

These recipes can be downloaded from this webpage:

http://marthadrummond.com/vegan-slow-cooker-cookbook-bonus/

I hope you enjoy them.

Martha

Other Cookbooks by Martha Drummond

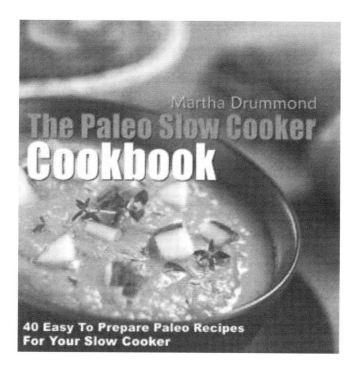

The Paleo Slow Cooker Cookbook

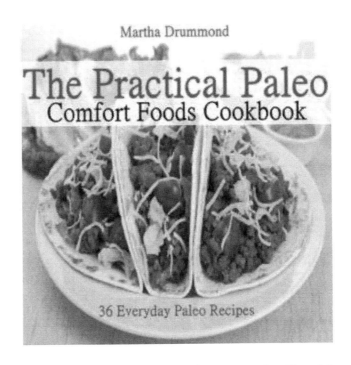

The Practical Paleo Comfort Foods Cookbook

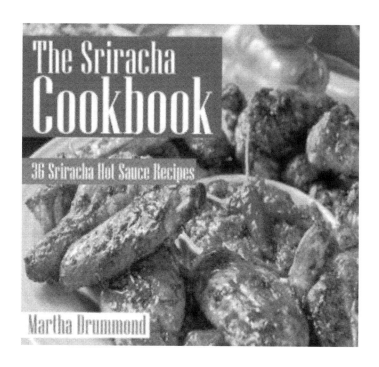

The Sriracha Cookbook

The Sriracha Vegan Cookbook

The Breakfast Sandwich Maker Cookbook

Printed in Great Britain
by Amazon